THE
LAST
DOLLAR

CREATING A POWERFUL AND EFFECTIVE MONETARY SYSTEM WITHOUT THE DOLLAR

PHIL TAYLOR-GUCK

RETHINK PRESS

First published in Great Britain in 2019 by Rethink Press
(www.rethinkpress.com)

Disclaimer
The views expressed in this book do not constitute financial
advice. The investment ideas discussed should never be used
without first assessing your own financial situation and
consulting a qualified financial advisor. Neither the author
nor the publisher can be held responsible for any losses that
may result from investments made after reading this book.

Contents

Introduction

These days, it is tempting to turn off the news, disconnect social media and keep away from the newsstands. There appears to be an endless diet of doom, from the global climate crisis and escalating trade wars, to a return to polarised and bitter politics. Sometimes you might feel better off in ignorance. Yet now, more than ever before, is exactly the time to sit up, take notice and get active. While many economists have *hinted* that we can expect to enter another slowdown period, the warnings are nothing like as loud as they need to be.

The reason for writing this book is to help you become informed ahead of a global financial crisis, which I believe is imminent. In fact, today we are facing the prospect of a global slowdown that could be completely different from any recessions that have gone before. Indeed, it could be different from any of the other economic crises we have witnessed in our lifetimes. The reason it will be tougher than anything that has gone before is because there is nothing the Bank of England, the Federal Reserve System, or any other central banks or regulators can do to stop it. Central banks will not be able to fall back on injecting liquidity – 'quantitative easing' – which was used to ease the pain of the downturns in 1998 and 2008. Quite simply, they have exhausted their ammunition. Whatever economic downturn happens is going to be deep and very painful indeed.

There are ample signs that we are entering an acute phase of economic pressure, a precursor to an impending recession. Taking centre-stage is the weak performance of the dollar. The 'Mighty Greenback' is no longer mighty at all. In fact, the dollar is in real trouble. We are seeing a massive global shortage of dollars. The impact on global liquidity is proving painful, particularly when taken against a backdrop of artificially inflated financial markets, the result of previous central bank attempts at protecting the status quo.

The vulnerability of the dollar does not spell bad news just for the citizens of the United States. It is a shrieking klaxon warning to everyone around the world, since the dollar is the global reserve currency. It is at the centre of *every* economy. Put simply, right now our futures depend upon it.

What is needed is a global solution – and fast. However, while those in power around the world are beginning to wake up to the problems we are facing and approaches are being raised and debated, any changes will be made at an achingly slow pace. It takes years to hammer out an international agreement (and any agreement here would involve many, many nations, some of which of are not traditionally keen to cooperate with one another). Even if they reach agreement, it can take further years to implement. The only time that there is any swift international cooperation is when there is a major global crisis, such as war, or a financial catastrophe: a situation no one wants.

One of the biggest problems is that the discussions are beginning at the wrong starting point. Everyone is focusing on bad debt. What very few people seem prepared to accept is that the problem facing us all now is not caused by the *existence* of bad debt. The problem lies within the easy-money policies that created the debt in the first place. The regulators are all desperately looking for a solution to the *wrong* problem.

What our leading economic powers should be scrutinising is the whole idea of elastic money. This concept emerged in the twentieth century, in the wake of the decision to abandon the gold standard and fixed exchange rates and tie world currencies to the Mighty Greenback. Espoused by economists such as Milton Friedman of the University of Chicago, the theory was that previous financial crises had been caused by overly tight monetary policy. Friedman pronounced that if banks were able to *create* money as needed to counteract the effects of recession, or to depress or boost demand for goods and services, that would be to everyone's benefit. Under this system, 'enlightened' central bankers could carefully calibrate the money supply to encourage real growth. No macroeconomic problem in the world could not be solved by judicious government spending and/or additional supplies of newly printed currency, or so the thinking goes.

As we have since discovered to our cost, these assumptions have a fatal flaw. The theory is based on assumptions that over-simplify the *real* world. Elastic money is entirely reliant on markets being efficient and activities being rational and measured. As we all know only too well, people are rarely rational where money is concerned. Greed always comes into play. The elastic money system depends far too much on trading partners complying with rules and populations trusting their leaders. But at times of stagnant growth, or out-of-control asset bubbles, or widening income disparity, or trade wars, these assumptions rapidly unravel.

Artificially manipulating currency can damage trade because it creates false signals. Distortions creep in because actual supply and demand cannot be properly read by the markets. Price distortions produce shortages and inflation. And the result? Well the clue to that lies in the truism that money's status is not conveyed by state action; it reflects *confidence*, relying on an unsaid pact between two parties making an exchange of money that they can both have confidence that the medium of exchange will accurately transfer value. In the past, this medium has been gold, silver, beads, even mackerel (some US prison inmates use the oily fish as a currency known as 'macks'). But confidence is fragile and easily lost. Right now, confidence in the dollar is rapidly evaporating.

In truth, 'economic stability' cannot be easily and consistently maintained by a system of elastic money. Outside events will eventually destroy whatever economic balance has been struck, and with it whatever has been heralded as the 'best way' to ensure a stable economy. It could be war, drought, hurricanes, or interruptions from innovations, from the railroad to the internet. No one can reliably predict all such events, *ergo* there is never a sure-fire way to guarantee stability. However, our continued attempts to do so often generate the very effects they are trying to prevent.

In this book, I have tried to shed some light on how we got to where we are today and what the potential outcomes might be, both for the dollar and for the world economy. I have not shied away from describing the possible outcomes of continuing down the present, dangerous course. The system of fluctuating fiat money, where successive US governments have allowed the manipulation of the value of the dollar with knock-on effects for the currencies tied to it, has forced a shift away from wealth creation to wealth destruction. Tens of millions of US citizens are already feeling a very real decline in their incomes and reduced financial circumstances. It is inevitable that more and more 'ordinary' US citizens will lose confidence in the dollar.

There is an urgent need for governments and regulators to stop repeating the same mistakes and to start appreciating classic monetary principles. Old-fashioned is not always a bad thing. As you will read here, the gold standard and a system of fixed exchange rates had a lot going for them. While there is no such thing as 'economic stability' and there will always be economic cycles to contend with, we can have *stable money*. It is only by embracing this idea that we will be able to stop the clumsy attempts by bureaucrats to tighten or loosen the economy having destructive consequences.

There are already strong signals that a modern gold standard, adapted for the twenty-first century global economy, might be an answer to a great many problems. Linking the dollar, or indeed any currency or basket of currencies, to gold, could well be the best way to achieve the monetary stability that we so badly need. There will be objectors to this idea. Indeed, a long line of economic experts have long dismissed the gold standard as a dinosaur best left in the past. I believe this view is based on ignorance of what it means and how it would work. Gold is far more flexible than people generally acknowledge. It is high time these misguided views were re-examined, and I have laid out the arguments carefully in this book.

The only way that we can possibly protect ourselves and our wealth is to wake up to what has been happening and to understand how we got here. Only then can we make proper plans for our future.

ONE

How Did We Get Here?

It is reasonable to not expect much fireworks and excitement from a group of central bankers and academic luminaries meeting for an annual symposium. Yet, while the central bankers' get-together in Jackson Hole in Wyoming towards the end of August 2019 did not offer edge-of-your-seat entertainment, it was the setting for probably one of the most important discussions in decades, which will profoundly affect everyone's future. And at the centre of it all? The prospects for the dollar.

For as long as most people can remember, the Mighty Greenback has been *the* global currency. In films, it is routinely the much-coveted reward in heists and drug deals from Mexico City to Moscow. Weary travellers arriving in Bangalore can count on the fact that, if they have not yet had time to take out any local currency, a taxi driver will be happy to take payment in dollars. It is even a natural part of our vernacular to express admiration; *you look a billion dollars tonight.* The dollar is everywhere. As of the first quarter of 2019, the dollar made up 61% of all known central bank foreign exchange reserves.[1]

That is all set to change. The days of the dollar as the dominant medium of exchange and international focal point are numbered. Those central bankers, sipping mineral water at Jackson Hole as they talked earnestly about global economics, were discussing nothing less than a regime shift. Until then, anyone speaking about the 'demise of the dollar' was usually dismissed as a crank. Now, renowned experts such as the Bank of England's Mark Carney were opening up to the possibility of just that. The Jackson Hole professionals were discussing turning their backs on the dollar altogether in favour of a more global monetary policy.

If this all sounds like fairly insignificant to you, rather akin to the chore of changing currency for a foreign holiday, think again. It represents a profound shift in global economics. More importantly, it signals that the authorities are only now waking up to the fact that we are on the edge of what might turn out to be a very high cliff for the majority of the world's population. Arguably, the fact that bankers have only now begun to recognise the possibility of the dollar crisis means we are already too late to stop a chain of potentially catastrophic events. Regulators, as we all know, are notoriously slow to react.

How did we get here?

As with so many things in economics, there are many contributing factors. For now though, let's focus on two key ones: firstly, the dollar's status as the world's reserve currency and how successive US governments have attempted to adjust things to maintain its dominance, with varying degrees of success; secondly, the emerging realisation that the role of paper money at the centre of our economic strategy no longer makes any sense. Indeed, paper money has been nothing short of a potentially highly destructive distraction for some years now.

The world's reserve currency

Let's begin with the dollar and briefly dart back in history to explain its growth in significance. The US Federal Reserve, the central bank of what is currently the world's largest economy and the provider of its leading paper currency, the dollar, started life in 1913. It was not long after this that the Fed, as it is often known, was first accused of interference, with economists claiming its policies were detrimental to the short- and medium-term prospects of the economy. The Great Depression that began in 1929 was said to be, at least in part, down to the Fed stepping in to fuel a credit boom.[2] The Fed's response in the wake of the financial crisis was also criticised for being inadequate.

Some commentators felt that it may even have prolonged the pain by not injecting money quickly enough.

There were further changes to the monetary infrastructure in the 1930s, including, crucially, President Roosevelt's decision to abandon the gold standard, thus breaking the link between the value of the dollar and the price of gold. He reasoned that 'the free circulation of gold coins is unnecessary, leads to hoarding, and tends to a possible weakening of national financial structures in times of emergency'.[3]

The gold standard had long been the unquestionable anchor of the monetary system. It was a promise that, if you had a dollar, you could take it to the government and trade it for a fixed amount of gold. It was not unique to the USA, either. All the key world economies relied on the same system. In fairness to Roosevelt, the gold standard had started to unravel prior to his move: the UK had abandoned it two years earlier. The Bank of England had reacted to panic amongst the population in response to the

UK depression of the 1920s which had meant there was a very real danger the Bank might run out of gold. Its strategy of ditching the gold standard created a ripple that ran round the world as people raced to exchange their paper money for gold before their governments did as the UK had done. Facing the mother of all bank runs, the US president stepped in and did the same as England, even though all but one of his economic advisors warned against it. And the net result? Well, when a government is not tied to gold, it has more tools at its disposal to steer the economy. It can, for example, adjust interest rates and 'control' inflation. Almost overnight, the future of our international balance sheets was suddenly much more vulnerable to the actions and fallibilities of individual economic advisors.

Fast forward just over a decade to the end of the Second World War. A conference of the Allied nations was urgently convened at Bretton Woods, New Hampshire just weeks after the D-Day landings. The goal was to find a way to stabilise foreign exchange rates and strengthen the internal monetary systems of the Allied countries at a time when everyone was just daring to start to think about the world after the war. Memories of the 1920s and 1930s were still very vivid, of nations heavily engaged in competitive devaluations in a bid to gain some export advantage over others in the dark days of the global depression. International trade had all but collapsed in the face of unpredictable exchange rates and tariff wars.

The declared aim of the Bretton Woods talks was to level the monetary playing field and guarantee the much-needed expansion of free trade. Accordingly, the Allies agreed rules for a new international monetary system based on fixed exchange rates, anchored by a US dollar convertible to gold. Bretton Woods established the role of the dollar as the premier reserve currency, replacing the British pound. A reserve currency is held in significant reserves by governments and institutions as a means of international payment and to support individual national currencies. Originally, such reserves held mostly gold and silver, but this postwar agreement expanded the acceptable reserves to include other currencies: the dollar was the premier one. At the time, the shift made perfect sense. In the confusion following the devastating global conflict, much of the world lay in ruins and the USA accounted for more than half of the combined economic output of the Great Powers (the USA, the UK, France, Germany, Italy, Austria, the Soviet Union and Japan).[4] It was the world's largest importer and main source of trade credit, so it made perfect sense to make the dollar the focal currency. Likewise, since America was the main source of foreign capital, it made sense that international financial transactions were conducted in the dollar. Other countries were encouraged to stabilise their currencies against the dollar and thereby committed to holding dollar reserves to be able to ride out fluctuations in case of any SNAFU in the foreign exchange markets.

While the Bretton Woods agreement represented another boost to the rise of the dollar, it was still linked to gold, albeit tenuously. Although the external values of foreign currencies were fixed in relation to the US dollar, that currency's value was, in turn, expressed in gold at the congressionally agreed price of $35 per ounce. There was, however, plenty of elbow room to take measures to adjust the economy as and when the authorities became alarmed that things were not going their way. Thus, in the 1960s, when US foreign aid and investment, as well as military spending, meant that dollars were flooding the world market, the USA realised it did not have enough gold to cover the volume of dollars in circulation worldwide. Presidents John F. Kennedy and then Lyndon B. Johnson adopted a series of measures to support the greenback and keep the Bretton Woods system on an even keel. They introduced disincentives to US citizens investing in other countries, restricted US banks from lending abroad and negotiated international monetary reform. Regardless, traders in foreign exchange markets, sensing the weakness, sold dollars in the belief that the US government would at some point have to devalue it. The strategy caused several runs on the dollar which, for obvious reasons, alarmed the US government. President Nixon stepped in to put a stop to the potential crisis. On 15 August 1971, he barred all main currencies from being converted into gold to 'protect the dollar from the attacks of international money speculators',[5] making the dollar a fiat currency. (Fiat currency is usually paper money; it is not backed or guaranteed by a commodity.)

Nixon's 1971 decision to suspend the system under which the dollar could be converted to gold had initially been mooted as a temporary measure, while supposed flaws in the Bretton Woods accord were addressed. The goal had been to produce a new monetary system to replace Bretton Woods, but the president was convinced by a group of economists who advocated floating exchange rates, rather than the fixed-rate system agreed at Bretton Woods. The proposed system, which became known as a 'free market' solution, must have sounded pretty attractive to the cash-strapped presidency. It could now operate without the need to balance budgets, or the discipline needed to make gold convertibility possible. The new solution fixed the 'problem' with gold, which is that there is a finite amount and the options for any new supplies are relatively fixed. Around 166,500 tonnes of the precious metal have been mined to date and just 2,500 tonnes are added to the stock each year.[6] While this rarity can drive gold's price up, it also means (in economic terms) that gold is relatively inelastic. Credit booms and busts are restricted by what is held in reserves. If banks lower their reserves too far, they need to cut back on lending, which means people have less money to invest and thereby extend the boom. Conversely, when the natural economic cycle flows around to a recession, there is little that can be done to soften or shorten any fall-out. Under a gold standard, the recession must therefore proceed unchecked, during which time whatever mis-alignments that have developed between the amounts being saved and those being invested are corrected and the imbalances are cleansed from the system.

The paper money system

Paper money operates entirely differently. (For clarification, I am referring to paper money as a concept here. I am well aware that most money has no physical form today; it is merely a book entry. We are firmly in the era of electronic money.) Paper money supplies are potentially infinite and very elastic, which is why Nixon embraced the idea so enthusiastically. Under this system, central banks can and do expand the money supply and adjust interest rates at will, in order to encourage extra investment and buoy up growth in the economy.

Back then, and to a great extent even now, no one appeared to question the very obvious flaw in the strategy: if exchange rates are determined by market forces, and therefore government intervention only affects them to an extent, where is the sense in allowing governments to build up huge foreign currency reserves? The rate at which one currency can be exchanged for another should be decided by market forces of supply and demand. If governments can accumulate reserves, which could be used to oppose or distort market perceptions, they can deliberately manipulate their own currencies to gain a competitive advantage.

These flaws were not acknowledged in 1971 when, at a stroke, the entire world shifted to a paper money standard. Money could now be created out of nothing, at no cost and with no limits. This changed everything.

In the free-for-all following Nixon's decision to opt for *no* monetary system, nations got quite used to manipulating the exchange rate to meet strategic objectives that were wholly unconnected with the money supply. Certain nations dabbled with deliberate currency devaluation in order to boost exports; others nudged their currency upwards to encourage foreign investment. Central banks adopted a leading role, becoming main players in audacious currency adjustments. It is not manipulation, they could argue, but simply the *consequence* for the *exchange rate* of achieving their economic objectives.

Naturally, misalignments began to arise between the amounts saved and the amounts invested. However, this misalignment was essentially allowed to continue unchecked (and indeed still is). Central banks apparently do not see the need to take action to correct any imbalances in the system, because they believe that the 'efficient market' will eventually do this for them, and by printing more money and raising or lowering interest rates they hope to control the flow. The ratio between savings and investments quickly got vastly out of synch, but perhaps no one really minded, because there was plenty to go round. Recessions are still inevitable, though, because the artificial booms that arise now and again, such as the dot com bubble of 1994–2000, cannot realistically continue forever. However, the thinking goes that recessions' impact can be kept down by injections of money, which can also shorten the duration of a downturn. Thanks to this far more elastic system, credit cycles have been extended considerably and slumps that have occurred have been relatively short-lived. The problem is (and it is a problem that has hardly been raised until now), when will the much needed corrections occur? Tough, but necessary, adjustments to saving versus investment price distortions are still needed. Left unchecked, these distortions will only ever get bigger with time.

None of this is to say the gold standard that preceded the transfer to fiat money was a perfect system. In the interests of balance, it should be said that there have always been drawbacks to this way of running the economy. As we saw in the early part of the twentieth century, people hoard gold during times of uncertainty. If money is tied to gold, less gold in circulation means less money is available to support day-to-day transactions and economic activity can drop, or stagnate. Also, gold does experience the odd shock and periods of rapid inflation, when new discoveries are made such as the California Gold Rush of the 1840s and 50s. Economists will tell you that unpredictable increases in the money supply caused by such events are more disruptive than the 'controlled' increases put in place by central banks, who control the injection of money into the economy. All of which brings me neatly to the question of just how effective these paper-money-based stimuli have actually been in averting or controlling financial disaster.

Banks and markets

It is only now beginning to be recognised that when central bank interference becomes the norm, this brings problems of its own. Commercial bankers have grown to *expect* bail-outs when things do not go to plan and place their market bets accordingly. With that safety net beneath them, they make ever-more ambitious bets (why wouldn't they?), which in turn can have greater negative impact if the cards do not fall as hoped. (And, as we all know, the cards do not arrive every time they are wanted.) What does this mean? Well, those imbalances that are part and parcel of the paper money system are just getting wider.

While it is fashionable to lay the blame for most economic woes at the door of reckless commercial bankers, they are not the only ones increasing the imbalance in our monetary systems. Central banks do not just expand the supply of money to counter economic threats; some also adjust the supply to meet political goals.

Now, you may say, this is nothing new. Money has always been a tool of the state, and 'the markets' are a fairly new idea. In other words, a country's rulers choose the money of account and impose taxes, fines and fees. With the shift towards paper money, though, governments have opportunity to create it, rather than having to raise it from their subjects.

Political leaders who are elected after promising economic growth, or reducing unemployment, or clamping down on inflation, only have a short time to make good on their pledges. The pressure is on to make meaningful shifts and, if the market is left to its own devices, these shifts may not happen naturally within the given target time. So, governments frequently need injections of new money to make the magic happen. What has changed? These artificial injections of money now routinely occur as part of the political cycle in several leading economies. Sometimes the money supply is expanded faster than at other times, but the result is the same: the money supply is continually, artificially, expanded. There is probably no leader in power who would not be able to give you a dozen reasons why they have had to do so. Many of the reasons will be creditable. Even so, you do not need to be a financial genius to work out that this cannot be sustainable in the long term. The entire monetary system is getting more and more distorted.

Let us not forget that the world monetary system is underpinned by the dollar, the premier worldwide reserve currency. The world can no longer ignore the growing mass of evidence that the monetary system is now so out of balance that it has become unsustainable. This was the reason why central bankers made this the focus of their annual conference in Jackson Hole. It was not the economic imbalances created by paper money that dominated their conversations, though. It was the dominance of the US dollar, which is making a difficult situation a whole lot worse.

TWO

The Global Economy Changes Everything

At face value, the dollar's position as the world's strongest currency looks unassailable. In 2010, around $580 billion were in circulation worldwide – in banknotes, not book entries,[7] representing 65% of *all* dollars at that time. More than one-third of the world's gross domestic product comes from countries that peg their currencies to the greenback.[8] Around 90% of foreign exchange trading is related to the dollar.[9] For anyone who is still not convinced, cast your mind back to the 2008 financial crisis which highlighted just how dominant the dollar has become. Banks outside America held $27 trillion. The Fed had to increase its dollar swap line so that the world's banks did not run out of dollars in those desperate days, with banks collapsing one after another.

This global dollar supremacy is all a legacy of that postwar Bretton Woods conference, when the Allied nations hammered out an agreement with one eye firmly on the goal of rebuilding the world's shattered infrastructure as quickly as possible. They needed to encourage economic growth to achieve this aim and the dollar provided an obvious answer. Today though, the world has moved on. What made sense more than seventy-five years ago does not seem quite so pertinent today. The US share of global exports is 14%; behind China (17%) and the EU (16%).[10]

Globalisation, liberalisation and market abuse

America is less dominant economically than it was in the postwar era. After a period of recovery after 1944, Europe bounced back and then so did Japan. Most recently, markets such as China and India have gained considerable ground. Central to the shift is the so-called 'death of distance' brought about by the ongoing transport and communications revolution. Breakthroughs in containerisation in the 1970s sparked the beginning of China's move to dominance as the new workshop of the world. Goods could be made there far more cheaply than elsewhere and then shipped anywhere on the globe. Meanwhile, India has become a new global services hub thanks to the invention of fibre optics and broadband. Earnings per capita (gross domestic product – GDP – divided by the total population) have risen in these new industrial powerhouses, and now seriously challenge the might of the USA. All of this is quite logical since there is no reason why US productivity should greatly exceed that of the rest of the world. Today, thanks to profound changes in the global economy and shifts in political, social and institutional structures, the dollar's share of global transactions is a great deal larger than America's share of global GDP.

Not surprisingly, some significant disparities have emerged. Swiss banks that accept deposits in *Swiss francs*, yet make foreign loans in *US dollars* as customers request, now face some very real implications for their profits if the exchange rate moves against them. That risk can be managed via hedging: but even hedging might be judged a rather unfair cost. After all, American banks that make loans in dollars and receive dollar deposits do not need to hedge their own currency. Manufacturers that send goods abroad are subject to the same imbalance. An Italian engineering firm that exports machine tools to China and receives payment in dollars would be within its rights to be frustrated by the additional costs of converting dollars back to euros. It is a cost the firm has no choice but to bear, though, because it needs the euros to pay its workforce and to purchase the materials to fill the next order. Just to add to the mismatch, under ever-increasing global trade, this Italian engineering firm will be competing against engineering firms from the USA. These US companies have the built-in competitive advantage of receiving their payments in dollars, the very currency they need to settle their debts and pay their workers.

We have seen again and again how dollar dependence can create spikes of panic, too. When US interest rates rise, money is sucked back into the USA and into dollars. The same thing happens when US investors feel nervous and become risk-averse. This has nothing to do with the actions of other countries, but can have a profound impact on those countries' domestic economies. In August 2018, a single tweet by President Trump, announcing that the USA would double the tariffs on imports of Turkish steel, caused Turkey's lira to fall more than 20% against the dollar.[11] A further unwelcome knock-on effect was a stampede by investors out of emerging market currencies everywhere.

The cost to America of producing its money is negligible. The Bureau of Engraving and Printing can churn out $100 bills at the cost of a couple of cents. If, however, another country wants to get its hands on that $100 bill, it has to provide $100-worth of goods or services. The term for this is *seignorage*, which dates back to medieval times, when the lord of the manor, or *seigneur*, would be given precious metal by his sovereign with which to coin money for the sovereign, and be allowed keep some of that metal for himself. In modern terms, think of it as follows: for every $1 billion of currency that circulates the world outside the USA, someone, somewhere, has had to provide the USA with $1 billion of goods and services. This does not look like a very fair arrangement to the international market and everyone knows it.

As if giving goods and services, plus being at a trading disadvantage, were not enough, there is also the question of straight money payments to the USA, thanks to the dollar's dominance. Foreign banks and firms do not simply deal in US currency. Many also hold US treasury bills and bonds, which are more convenient to handle thanks to the dollar's pre-eminence. Treasury bills and bonds pay interest, but the widespread ownership of them is also to the advantage of the US Treasury and the government agencies that issue them. It is estimated that foreign banks hold bonds worth $5 trillion and add to them every year.[12]

The hedge fund billionaire and philanthropist George Soros has an interesting take on the dollar situation, which he outlined in his book *The New Paradigm for Financial Markets*.[13] His view of the credit crisis of 2008 was that the debt bubble followed a shift in the early 1980s, when markets opened up through globalisation and market fundamentalism. Soros says that debt began to grow uncontrollably because the USA routinely abused its position as the premier reserve currency. From its place at the centre of global trade, it had long been taking advantage of the shift towards the 'magic of the markets' as once hailed by Ronald Reagan, and greatly benefited from the liberalisation. At the root of the problem was the fact that the US markets were not affected by many of the rules that the International Monetary Fund (IMF) has inflicted on smaller, developing nations, governing the size of deficits they could run. The upshot? The USA comfortably slipped into the habit of living well beyond its means as large amounts of cash flowed into the the country to pay for its lifestyle.

While commentators have been aware of the glaring inconsistencies and unfairness in the system for a long time, little has been done. Part of the problem is: shifting the balance cannot necessarily be done unilaterally. The entire world has signed up to the dollar and it would be a brave country indeed that tried to lead the charge away from that. For a long while, dollar discontents could at least comfort themselves with the knowledge that, with everything going OK and economies growing, there was little urgency to force what will inevitably be a hugely disruptive change. Growth was never going to last indefinitely, though.

Unhappy subjects and asset bubbles

The clear problem that is embedded within the current system is: when you use another country's currency, you are to a great degree subject to its monetary policy. As mentioned above, the implications of this were laid bare during the 2008 financial crisis, which essentially began in the USA and then dragged the rest of the world down with it. In the run-up to the credit crunch, the USA had been running current account deficits of up to 6%. In the background, more vulnerable emerging markets had been building dollar reserves as their economies grew, and so providing a cheap source of finance for the US deficit, whether they wanted to or not. Poorer households in the developing world were essentially propping up the American boom. When the boom got out of hand, millions of Americans went further than simply living beyond their means and into new and outrageous spendthrift territory: ordinary people began taking out mortgages on multiple properties, or several mortgages on the same property. When credit dried up, institutions tried to call these mortgages in, sometimes found no property they could repossess (because it 'belonged' to several other institutions), and at other times found themselves stuck with assets worth a fraction of what they had lent. This had knock-on effects for other countries, whose reserves plunged in value along with the dollar.

The 2008 financial crisis highlighted two further distinct problems with dollar dominance. It is not just that what might work in monetary policy terms for the USA does not always work for another country. There is also the question of an awkward compromise between an individual country's policy and what the USA is doing with the dollar. Conducting monetary and fiscal policy with one eye on the USA, rather than focusing 100% on what their own economy needs, is not a good way to run any country.

But, after putting up with the inadequacies of dollar dominance for so long, what has brought us to a crunch today? The answer lies in the policies pursued in the aftermath of the 2008 crisis. This was when the term quantitative easing (QE) entered the mainstream. QE is where central banks purchase assets as a way of pumping new money into the economy in order to stimulate it, and is a mechanism that is traditionally used when other policies, such as cutting interest rates, fail. Between 2008 and 2016, the Federal Reserve in the USA printed $12.3 trillion.[14] They were not alone in this. In the UK, the Bank of England spent £435 billion buying back government debt in a programme of QE.[15] However, as the global premier reserve currency, US QE was always going to have an impact beyond its own borders.

QE is a bit of a blunt instrument, particularly when used for a prolonged period. Every time you add a dollar or pound to the economy by 'printing money', it devalues what is already in circulation. Something that central bankers were most fearful of was that all the extra dollars sloshing around the system would eventually create an asset bubble, which is, of course, exactly what has happened. (An asset bubble is where the price of assets, such as stocks, bonds, property or commodities, rises rapidly without being supported by any underlying fundamentals, such as rising demand or proven supply, to justify the spike.) In fact, QE did not just create *one* asset bubble, it played a role in creating *multiple* asset bubbles. Virtually all of the extra money that has been printed has found its way to the stock market. Stocks are now enjoying the longest bull market in history, with the US s&p500 nearly quadrupling in value since 2009.[16] Meanwhile, the US corporate debt bubble is growing with $1.3 trillion in leveraged loans, $1.2 trillion in junk bonds and $3 trillion of investment-grade corporate debt, just one notch above junk.[17] The bubble is not just in stocks and bonds, though. The price of US real estate continues to rise relentlessly. In 2017, the average price of a family home soared at a rate 32% higher than inflation. That is not far off the 2005 level, when properties were 35% overvalued. While new home sales fell 22% between November 2017 and September 2018, home prices overall are still showing no significant signs of following suit.[18]

Aside from these obvious asset bubbles, there is another piece of alarming evidence that the American economy is actually anything but solid. Student loans do not support the buoyant headlines that trumpet the USA's 'booming' economy and record low employment: loan defaults doubled between 2003 and 2011 and 40% of borrowers are expected to fall behind on their loans by 2023.[19] The outstanding student loan balance is forecast to reach $2 trillion by 2022, with a large portion unlikely to ever be repaid. Covering these losses will add hundreds of billions to federal deficits for years to come. This is before you even get to the fact that, with more than 40% of the balances owned by people under 30, these graduates simply will not be able to spend money on houses or cars and, just as significantly, they may not be able to save and invest.

There is pressure to normalise things, but how far do you go? Not too far, if the Fed's reaction is anything to go by. Adjusting interest rates is one of the tools that they have at their disposal, but they have been reluctant to do anything drastic. Any interest rate rises have been gradual, so as not to cause disinflation, or reduce job creation or shock the markets. In reality, this translates to rate hikes of just 0.25% four times a year, but even these small rises have often been put on hold or postponed. According to the Fed's public pronouncements, the priority is to keep the

US economy growing with maximum employ-ment, while also keeping inflation in check. *Asset bubble, what asset bubble?* This dove-like policy may well have been influenced by the bombastic public commentary from President Trump, who has long complained that rate increases are causing unnecessary harm to the economy and markets. However, the outcome is the same: the asset bubbles are continuing to inflate unchecked.

Son of QE: QT

What has particularly irked many international governments is that dollar dominance has actually *grown* since the 2008 financial crisis. Then, just to make things even more frustrat-ing, the currency is now becoming more scarce, exacerbating an already difficult situation. The Fed has switched to a policy of quantitative tightening (QT) and is now removing dollars from the world's financial system as part of efforts to tighten the USA's domestic monetary policy and to begin unwinding their balance sheets, which have been artificially inflated thanks to QE. Instead of buying assets from the Treasury, central banks are dumping the assets they bought under QE back on the market. QT tightens the money supply and is a process that will inevitably have a destabilising effect. Ironically, this attempt to stop another global credit crunch has made dollars harder to come by. As you can imagine, this is not an ideal state of affairs for countries that are heavily reliant on dollar stocks. In 2017, the banks of Japan, Germany, France and the UK held more liabilities in dollars than in their own currencies.[20]

The resulting scramble for dollars by international banks has made them more expensive to borrow. There is plenty of evidence that it is having an impact. French lender Société Générale recorded its worst trading day of the year in December 2016 and blamed the dollar crisis in its annual report.[21] Hardly surprisingly, it is now deploying countermeasures to diversify sources of dollar funding across markets and types of investor.

Another real issue with the Fed's ongoing adjustments is that they put America out of step with countries that have their currencies pegged to the dollar, either on a formal or informal basis. How do these countries deal with the current situation? Should they break the peg, close their capital accounts or devalue their own currencies? Step back and imagine how disruptive the various Fed policies have been to anyone reliant on the dollar. In the period between 2008 and 2014, the Fed printed around $4 trillion of new money. It is now embarking on a strategy to destroy £2 trillion even more quickly. Inevitably, this is going to have a negative impact. If the Fed feels the need to defend itself (and it does not) it might assert that there is a strong argument for tightening the dollar, thanks to its confidence that the USA is experiencing a period of solid growth.

The very obvious fault lines in the global monetary system are beginning to show signs of great strain. Confidence in the dollar had been shaken long before the USA began aggressively tightening its money supply to improve domestic conditions. Now, as we will see in the next chapter, there is more urgency than before to reduce the imbalance. The gulf between what

US policymakers want and what individual countries feel is in their own best interests is widening to proportions that can no longer be easily ignored.

THREE

We've Reached A Critical Point

The failures of the paper money system have been evident ever since the first recorded use of paper money, which can be traced back to China as early as AD1000, coinciding with the development of paper, ink and printing systems. Paper money systems began with the Southern Song Dynasty and were subsequently introduced by the Jin Dynasty, the Yuan Dynasty and during the early period of the Ming Dynasty. In each case, paper money was introduced to raise revenues for the state; however, every time, runaway inflation eventually rendered the paper money worthless. The collapse of each paper money system coincided with the collapse of the dynasty that introduced it, or their conquest by the next in line and so the cycle continued. It was the Ming Dynasty that brought an end to the boom and bust, by switching to commodity money, spelling an end to paper money in China from 1500.

The Western world obviously did not get the memo about the successive failures of paper money and, for the past four centuries, has repeated many of the mistakes that had been already exhaustively rehearsed in ancient China. Over and over again. There has been a succession of failed paper money regimes, including a few in the North American colonies in the sixteenth, seventeenth and eighteenth centuries, and a couple of short-lived ones in France from 1716 to 1720, and 1775 to 1781. It was in the twentieth century though, that our love affair with paper money really seemed to take hold. Despite an early failure in Germany, with its doomed *Papiermark* system of 1914 to 1923, successive central banks decided that paper money was the way to go. Since then, as previously noted, there has been a succession of shifts away from commodities like gold and towards placing greater power in the hands of governments.

And still the paper money collapses keep coming. Currencies such as the North American continentals, French assignats and German Reichsmarks are now consigned to the history books, largely forgotten by all but avid coin collectors. The pound and dollar are the longest surviving currencies still in use, but it is clear that these currencies are closely linked with economic volatility, financial instability and rising inflation, and that goes for the dollar in particular. Indeed, the fact that we have seen a succession of currency disasters (The Great Depression, the dot-com boom and bust, the credit crunch) is no coincidence. *'But it's OK, we're controlling inflation,'* paper money fans will say. Except we are not. The twentieth century produced more inflation than any other century for which we have records. In fact, it produced 29 hyperinflations.[22] A hyperinflation is defined as a monthly rise in prices of 50% or more.

Despite all the evidence, fans of paper money still insist it is the best possible system. In 2002, Ben Bernanke, then a Federal Reserve governor, declared that 'under a paper-money system, a determined government can always generate higher spending and hence positive inflation'.[23] As we have already seen, what this prolonged central bank interference is actually achieving is the equivalent of kicking a ball into the long grass. Printing money, or restricting its supply, can only ever cover up the symptoms of a crisis and postpone the eventual crash. Even more worryingly, it also contributes to making the underlying problems worse, which will in turn make the eventual fall-out worse.

Comments like Bernanke's encourage a widespread complacency that, if an economic issue should arise, a few well-placed tweaks will always correct it. This is dangerously over simple. But the root causes of the danger signals we see today go far deeper than the successive US policies that have been introduced to correct imbalances and that are actively sabotaging the market. The fact is, there is no way to avoid the final collapse of the boom that has been brought about by excessive credit expansion.

Trade wars

You do not need to look very far to see that the dollar crisis is now accelerating hard. At the core of the problem is the fact that the US federal budget deficit is growing much faster than expected. Thanks to President Trump's tax cuts and spending policies, the USA is borrowing heavily. The gap between what the US government brings in through taxes and other revenue sources, and what it spends, has widened to $960 billion for the 2019 fiscal year.[24]

The introduction of trade tariffs against China by the USA have added to the problem. The tariffs were first mooted by Trump in June 2016 during his campaign for the presidency, amid strong rhetoric about levelling the playing field with China. True to his word, Trump signed off on tariffs in March of the following year. Since then, after trade talks apparently broke down, there have been a succession of tit-for-tat tariffs.

As everyone knows, Beijing is not inclined to take any threat lying down. To date, China has retaliated to everything the USA has thrown at it. Underlying the nervousness about the tariff war are widespread fears that the spat could escalate into a more active conflict, say if the USA were to adjust its policy towards rogue states such as North Korea or Iran, which would anger China still further. This anger could drive China into deciding to up the ante by using finance as a weapon. Chinese agencies hold $1.1 trillion of US government securities, which represents 7% of total US government borrowing (this is down from a peak of 14% in 2011).[25] If it were to dump a significant proportion of these assets, this would destabilise world financial markets and drive interest rates higher because as soon as other investors realised what was happening, they would rush to do the same. It would create a spike in borrowing costs for the US government. The result of this abrupt and jarring move? The dollar would plummet.

Clearly, this is a move that China is no hurry to make. A dive in US bond prices would both affect the sale price China could obtain, and bring down the value of the remaining US Treasury holdings that it decided to hang on to – both ways, its own reserves would be hit hard. Any deterioration in the US economy would also be deeply felt in China, since a fifth of China's exports head that way. Plus, China uses its bond holdings as a tool to stabilise the yuan, so this would be a bit of an own goal. All that said: it is a tool Beijing could use and no one can be entirely sure that they would not, if pushed hard enough. The possibility is certainly enough to make world markets, central banks and governments very nervous indeed.

As tensions between Beijing and Washington continue to rise, the IMF has reduced the growth forecasts in its *World Economic Outlook* (WEO) for 2019 and 2020.[26] It had already done so in response to the stalling of global economic momentum thanks to weaker financial performances across the world. The Congressional Budget Office (CBO) predicts that the US deficit will continue to rise. By 2029, the US National Debt will reach its highest level as a share of the economy since the end of the Second World War.[27] Not surprisingly, the financial markets are hugely jittery about the US-China trade dispute, fearing it could develop into a full-scale currency war. On 5 August 2019, stocks plunged, with the Dow Jones Industrial Average falling by more than 766 points (2.9%) and London's FTSE100 Index by around 180 points (2.5%),[28] after Trump unleashed a Twitter tirade against China. In response, the People's Bank of China (PBOC) allowed the yuan to weaken below the seven-yuan-to-one-dollar level, making Chinese goods cheaper for overseas buyers. This move rattled the markets. It was a sign the trade war was morphing into a currency war. The dollar index, which measures the dollar against a basket of currencies, was more than 1% lower as a result. Investors are anticipating devaluations in the yuan and, at some point, the dollar. There are few commentators and analysts that now believe there is any prospect of a good resolution to this dispute.

Just to unsettle things still further, the international trade war intensified in 2018, when President Trump started charging levies on the imports of steel and aluminium from key allies, including the European Union. The EU hit back, imposing retaliatory tariffs on everything from bourbon whiskey to orange juice. Then, in April 2019, President Trump upped the ante still further by announcing proposals to impose tariffs on around $11 billion worth of goods from the European Union.[29]

From trade wars to sanctions

What does the spate of trade wars mean for the future of the dollar? If you break down the potential scenarios, the prospects are not good. A trade war is, after all, essentially a dialogue between two nations where each party seeks to undermine the other. This cannot be good news when you take into account the underlying problems with the dollar which we have already discussed here.

There are plenty of examples from history to show us how damaging aggressive tariffs can be. Amid all the fall-out of the Great Depression, world trade plummeted by 25% after individual countries circled the wagons and introduced strict protectionist policies. In the aftermath, economies around the globe faltered under rising debt and weak domestic currencies.

Another damaging phenomenon associated with trade wars is currency devaluation. Countries in the midst of trade wars can seek to mitigate the pressure felt on their exports by devaluing their domestic currencies. It is a way of offsetting the negative impact of increased tariffs on goods and services and protecting the market share of exports. We have already seen China try this.

The potential fall-out from trade wars is not the only policy that points to an increasingly diminished role for the dollar. Sanctions have become a much favoured tool in US foreign policy. These commercial and financial penalties are applied for a variety of military, political and social ends, but in America's case economic sanctions appear to have gained most traction in recent times. Indeed, it would be fair to say that the use of economic sanctions by the USA, which may include various forms of trade barriers, tariffs and restrictions on financial transactions, has exploded in the twenty-first century. As of May 2019, the USA had nearly 8,000 sanctions in place,[30] ranging from sanctions on individuals such as Mexican drug lord Joaquin 'El Chapo' Guzman, to others on companies such as Cubacancun Cigars and Gift Shops, to still others covering entire governments and regimes, such as Iran and the Islamic Revolutionary Guard Corps.

America's use of sanctions is nothing new. They are a useful tool of influence. Rather than going to war to achieve a goal, sanctions aim for a similar desired affect by threatening cash flow. The thinking goes that when foreign governments find that it is difficult to access money or move it around, they will generally come around to making the required adjustments. The fact that the dollar is the premier reserve currency and the USA holds an important status at the centre of the global economy adds to the pressure.

As with any type of threat, it is only possible to use sanctions a certain number of times. There will come a day when sanctions cease to intimidate. They will have been used too often to have the same level of impact. It is not just that, though. The unilateral use of economic sanctions has not been well received by many of America's closest allies. Why? Because sanctions may hurt their own economic interests. Restrictions on doing business with Russia and Iran are not universally liked. What is even less popular is the idea that economies outside America are restrained from going it alone, thanks to the ongoing dominance of the Mighty Greenback.

In recent times we have seen a growing push-back against US economic sanctions, which is yet another sign of the waning influence of the dollar. In just one example, the governments of France, Germany and the UK have developed a special purpose vehicle to enable European businesses to maintain non-dollar trade with Iran, effectively circumventing US sanctions.

When it comes to the accelerating fall in status of the Mighty Greenback, there is another problem, closer to home this time: President Trump's much vaunted domestic tax cuts. All the evidence is suggesting that, far from paying for themselves, the tax cuts are actually driving up the US trade deficit, and to levels not seen since the financial crisis. Far from safely tucking away their extra cash in savings schemes, US consumers have been happily spending the windfall. That is not all. Many of the additional bonds that the US Treasury is issuing to dampen the rising deficit are being bought by foreign investors. This increases capital flows into the USA, which is good in the short term; but the interest on those bonds is leaving the USA, which contributes to the deficit.

Those who still champion tax cuts point in the direction of a similar move by an earlier president, Ronald Reagan. The tax cuts that characterised Reaganomics were followed by robust real growth that continued for the following decade. However, what these commentators fail to acknowledge is that the Reagan tax cuts followed *six successive quarters* of negative growth, which constitutes a very different starting point from today's rather bubbly markets. It is quite probable the Reagan era would have experienced boom times without the tax cuts. In the current US scenario, the economy is close to full capacity. Wages are fairly static, but unemployment is very low.

Drowning in debt

What is even more worrying is the fact that Reagan and his tax cuts enlarged the US debt-to-GDP ratio from 35% to 55% during his administration, a near 60% hike. Today, the USA's debt-to-GDP ratio is at 109%.[31] If Trump's tax policies caused a similar 60% hike, America would be staring down the barrel of a debt-to-GDP ratio of around 175%. This is close to the 181% debt-to-GDP ratio which has mired Greece in a deep economic crisis for more than a decade. The CBO has already admitted that the tax cuts will *temporarily* increase GDP growth above the US economy's productive capacity. It is inevitable that the monetary crisis surrounding the dollar will come to a head long before the US debt-to-GDP ratio reaches such dizzying levels. With the dollar such an important part of global commerce, it is not in anyone's interests to see it sink under a mountain of debt. The time for intervention cannot be that far off. The US debt problem is only getting worse.

It is not just the unpaid-for tax cuts, the tariff wars, the sanctions that are driving the dollar to a critical point. The burgeoning dollar crisis could not have occurred at a worse time. The US population is rapidly ageing, which has put us on the threshold of a major demographic crisis. The baby boom generation – those postwar children born between 1946 and 1964 – are now at retirement age. In a disastrous coincidence, this enormous population bubble coincides with a time when the US birth rate is at its lowest point ever. Let us focus on what that means in America, since we are looking at the future of the dollar. According to a US Census Bureau report, by the year 2035 78 million US citizens will be aged 65 and older, compared with 76 million under the age of 18. As the population ages, the old-age dependency ratio (the balance between older adults and adults of working age) is shifting. In Los Angeles County, for example, there are currently 5.2 working adults for each retired person, but in 20 years that figure will drop to 2.9.[32]

The rapid ageing of the population suggests that debt and deficits are set to accelerate at an even more rapid rate in the coming years, because a smaller proportion of the population will be working and paying taxes to support a larger proportion that are retired and, even if not drawing benefits, using public facilities. Rising debt will slow economic growth, which will in turn slow the growth in wages, and hence government income. Another significantly unwelcome consequence of the rising National Debt will be the probable rise in interest rates. As the US government is forced to issue more bonds to cover its debts and required spending, lenders will demand higher interest rates because their investment will need to compete with other investment opportunities elsewhere, and because the size of the US debts make it an increasingly poor credit risk. This will be hugely damaging because low interest rates have been protecting the USA (and the dollar) for so long. The CBO projects that annual interest payments will accelerate from $389 billion in 2019, to $914 billion by 2028. Net interest costs will total nearly $7 trillion over the next decade.[33] These numbers present a pretty bleak picture and what is worse is that they are based on government estimates, which generally present the rosiest picture possible. In theory, things could actually get a lot worse.

The impact of sharply rising US interest rates will be catastrophic for international trade, too. When the Fed raises rates, strengthening the dollar, the currency exchange rates of other countries tend to weaken. Take emerging markets as a case in point, because they are particularly vulnerable to changes in interest rates. Many companies in emerging markets have fuelled their growth by borrowing in dollars and making repayments in stronger, local currencies. According to the Bank for International Settlements, the value of dollar-denominated bonds issued by non-bank emerging markets has doubled since 2008, from $509 billion to $1.1 trillion, on the back of historically low interest rates.[34] When interest rates rise, this will lead to a wave of corporate defaults as companies struggle to service their debts.

Closer to home, the strong dollar worsens terms of trade for American exporters, but perhaps more crucially, the rising cost of dollars makes international banks unwilling to lend for trade finance because of the increased cost of funding. This makes it hard for international businesses to access the working capital they need to pay foreign suppliers. The knock-on effect is shrinking supply chains and a reduction in trade volumes.

Shrinking global trade has negative implications for global growth and there will be losers everywhere you look. A number of countries have already been identified as being particularly vulnerable to losing foreign direct investment if investors retreat from them once interest rates rise. In such circumstances, Turkey, Brazil, India, South Africa and Indonesia would see their growth abruptly stall. Those same countries, and many others, would also see the value of their own currency drop. After a period in which emerging markets have experienced an appreciation in their currencies and leveraged that growth to borrow more and finance new initiatives, currency values will sink. Indeed, there are already signs that currency values are falling in expectation of interest rate rises.

Meanwhile, if interest rates should double, or triple, from the current low levels (to historically not-very-high levels) interest payments on America's huge (and growing) debt would soak up 20%, 30% or even 40% of its budget. Spending on national security would have to reduce, and on healthcare (do not forget there will be added pressure on the healthcare system as the population ages). This scenario alone has been enough to see off other, once power-ful, empires. In 1788, ahead of the Revolution, France was spending 62% of royal revenues on servicing its debt. In the years between the First and Second World Wars, the UK buckled under interest payments consuming 44% of its budget, making re-arming in the face of a renewed German threat very difficult indeed.[35]

There is little possibility of some economic self-healing miracle to kick in and help the dol-lar swim against the tide of capital corrections and market distortions. There certainly does not seem to be any credible US plan to restore the Federal budget to balance over the next five to ten years. Therefore, the only way the global economy can begin to properly recover and work to everyone's advantage is to move away from the dollar. Hardly surprisingly, this is a scenario which foreign governments are now taking very seriously indeed.

FOUR

The Parabolic Curve: Gradually, Then Suddenly

There's a famous passage in Ernest Hemingway's novel *The Sun Also Rises,* where a character describes how he went bankrupt in two ways – gradually, and then suddenly.

Perpetual progress has been the cornerstone of Western society for 150 years or more. Each generation feels secure in the understanding that they will be better off than their parents. There have been occasional interruptions to this feeling of security, such as two world wars and numerous other conflicts, plus a handful of significant financial crashes. In all cases, though, economies have appeared to bounce back and everything quickly appeared to be stronger than ever. And, for as long as most generations can remember, stability has been underpinned by the mighty dollar. For many it must seem inconceivable that the dollar will ever falter, let alone collapse.

History has shown us that when bubbles finally burst, they burst quickly. There is a diagram for what happens at the end of a bubble too: a parabolic curve. Think of a graph which shows a steady, straight, horizontal line that increases at a gradual gradient, then suddenly shoots up at nearly 90 degrees. That is the parabolic curve and that is when things get completely unsustainable. That is where the USA and its debt are moving. Gradually, then suddenly.

Debt is useful... up to a point

US debt has been on that gradual incline northwards, away from the horizontal, for a while now. The thinking went that this was OK. Debt is useful when you want to build roads, fight wars or improve healthcare. As long as that debt increases at a slower pace than the economy, and the debt-to-GDP ratio reduces, we believe it is sustainable. However, if debt growth begins to outpace economic growth, growing perhaps twice or three times as fast, everything rapidly goes out of synch. There will come a time when the rate of increase becomes utterly infeasible and the debt bubble will simply pop.

The US's debt-to-GDP ratio is at 109% and rising.[36]

The US will not go bankrupt, at least not in the Hemingway sense. It can still print money. But essentially, the situation as it is cannot continue for ever. The stark fact, which markets are beginning to recognise, is that the dollar's move away from being the reserve currency is inevitable. As noted in chapter 1, central banks and politicians around the world are beginning to imagine Plan B. After decades of the USA steadily building up debt, with no particular long-term plan to pay it off other than hoping creditors keep expanding or rolling over the debt, it is very clear we are nearing the end of the line. We have already seen global growth and earnings heading downwards and there are other clear indicators that the economy is slowing, too, such as an inverted US yield curve. This is a tool analysts often use to examine the strength of an economy. When ten-year bond yields dip below those of two-year bonds, so long-term returns are lower than short-term ones, this sometimes signals that growth is likely to slow in the near future. As far as the markets can tell, little is being done to address this threat.

What has changed today, though? Why is the curve beginning to grow steeper? After all, the world is used to an unbalanced system in which the USA accounts for just 10% of global trade, and 15% of global GDP, yet the dollar is used to price half of trade invoices and two-thirds of global securities. The international markets know they have long been at a disadvantage as they trade with one another, and lose out with costly currency exchanges. The answer to the 'why now' question lies in just one word: uncertainty. Markets have always known how to adjust to good news. They can pivot, try a new direction, switch out of stocks, any of several strategies. They can adjust well to bad news, too. Sure, there will be hiccups in the system, maybe even a short-term loss, but any recovery can be swift. Today, though, things are different. Markets are faced with the one element they dislike most: uncertainty. Markets react hostilely to uncertainty. If putting a price on a transaction becomes difficult, dealing costs go up.

When the USA was viewed as a responsible and reliable leader of the world economy, every nation was prepared to live with frustrations with the shortcomings of the dollar as a premier reserve currency. There was an awareness that the changes and growth in international trade meant that at *some point* something would have to give, but that point seemed a long way off. After all, untangling the dollar's role as the world's reserve currency is no easy task. Then, the worldwide trading environment shifted.

As already noted, the bruising dispute over trade and exchange rates between President

Trump and China has sent shock waves through the global economy. There has been a succession of retaliatory tariffs between Beijing and Washington, and it seems as though each time markets are told that talks are progressing towards agreement, more tariffs are imposed. But it is not just President Trump's very public spat with China that has made other countries finally face up to the fact that the markets needed to review the dollar's right to remain a reserve currency. It is his policy on Mexico.

As James Bullard, the President of the St Louis Federal Reserve, observed in a newspaper interview, President Trump's abrupt change of mind on Mexico signalled dire long-term consequences for investment generally.[37] Bullard was referring to a development in May 2019, when Trump had threatened to impose tariffs on the US neighbour, even though the two countries had recently negotiated a trade deal. This seemingly arbitrary, overnight change spooked markets. They realised they were now operating in a world where the USA could inflict unexpected trade surprises on partners with whom it already held agreements. For the markets this represented a huge shift. For the first time, they were dealing with an issue that monetary policy did not influence and therefore could not shift.

Moving to a post-dollar world

Market sentiment plays a crucial role in global economics. History has shown us that investors are erratic. After months (perhaps years) of uncertainty, investors may wake up one morning and decide that holding dollars is a losing proposition. If enough investors act on this sentiment, others will follow. Soon the herd will be running relentlessly away from the dollar. Its place as the premier reserve currency will have become untenable.

While there is currently no realistic mechanism for decoupling the dollar from the global economy, the end of the dollar's role as the premier reserve currency is no longer a theoretical event discussed only by academics and economists. The eventuality is being factored into the economic strategies of the world's leading nations.

When the bubble bursts and that parabolic curve starts to steepen, everyone wants to be prepared. Thanks to the acute interconnectedness of the global economy, there will be long-term consequences for everyone.

Early discussions have centred around creating a 'more global monetary policy'. In other words, a mechanism whereby central banks can cooperate more effectively in a way that is to everyone's advantage. (Subtext: and move away from being arbitrarily impacted by changes in US domestic policy.) At the moment, the potential approaches being raised are wide-ranging and there seem no limits to the proposals being put forward. There have even been hints by Bank of England governor Mark Carney that capital controls (limits on the amount of money that can be brought into and out of a country) might be necessary, albeit only in extreme circumstances.[38] This is surprising in itself, since generally capital controls are reserved for fragile emerging markets that are faced with severe market turmoil. To date, though, there is no consensus on the way forward as central banks battle to come up with a monetary policy that will counteract an increasingly gloomy trade outlook that they have an apparently diminishing amount of control over.

So far, the focus of discussions has been: what will replace the dollar as the premier reserve currency? Officials in China and the euro zone have not been slow to tout their currencies as credible alternatives and have indeed been doing so for two or three years. The Chinese made serious grounds in its campaign in 2016, when its renminbi was added to the IMF's Special Drawing Rights basket, taking its place beside the dollar, euro, yen and pound sterling. Two years later, the renminbi was also introduced as a numeraire (an item or commodity acting as a measure of value, or a standard for currency exchange) in commodity markets when crude oil futures began trading in the Shanghai International Energy Exchange.

Europe also is actively looking for opportunities to expand the role of its currency, the euro. In his 2018 annual programme address, former European Commission President Jean-Claude Juncker laid out the EU's stall when he told the

European Parliament that it was 'absurd' that 80% of European energy imports, worth €300 billion a year, should be settled in dollars.[39]

Of course, switching from one reserve currency to another is not a step to be taken lightly. The disruption will be enormous. It will take time and be hugely traumatic. Plus, it is only really kicking the ball into the long grass once more. Whether global trade is priced in dollars, renminbi or the euro, the vulnerabilities to the system are still present.

The IMF has mooted the idea of using cryptocurrencies as a digital version of the former gold standard. Indeed, the Swedish central bank is already investigating the possibility of a digital supplement to cash, called the e-krona. Singapore is also experimenting, in this case with cross-border payments using a digital Singapore dollar.

While there are some similarities between cryptocurrency and gold, since they are both a store of value separated from the official money system, and the supply of Bitcoin is constrained to a maximum of 21 million coins at present, this becoming the new type of gold standard seems doubtful. One of the best known cryptocurrencies, Bitcoin, has been dismissed as 'a fraud' by influential JP Morgan chief executive Jamie Dimon, while Warren Buffett has predicted 'with certainty' that it will come to a 'bad ending'.[40] Aside from fears about the reliability of Bitcoin and possible vulnerabilities, there is the question of how much support it would receive from the USA. The USA may be keen to solve its present problems, but it seems highly unlikely the country would be willing to sign up to anything that would mean entirely letting go of its influence over global financial markets.

Another option could be an entirely new worldwide currency pegged to a basket of commodities. Reserves could be held in individual currencies, but payments for international trade could be calculated and settled according to the anchor unit. This would move the incentives for damaging currency wars and devaluations. Numerous technical issues have already been raised about such an arrangement, though, which might take several years to iron out. As already noted here, we do not have the luxury of time right now.

While central banks grapple with alternatives, there are already warning signs of defensive shifting away from the dollar. IMF data reveals that, in the second quarter of 2019, the dollar share of foreign reserves has fallen to its lowest level since the end of 2013 ($6.79 trillion, or 61.63% of allocated reserves). The share of foreign exchange reserves in the euro and the Chinese yuan (the name of the unit in which renminbi transactions are denominated) have increased from the previous quarter. Meanwhile the Japanese yen's share of reserves grew to its largest in nearly two decades.[41] All the signs are that central banks around the world are trying to plan ahead by actively diversifying their reserves.

In a further signal that nations are distancing themselves from the dollar, there are innovative moves to put different currencies centre stage. China has introduced swaps with participating countries to promote the use of the yuan/renminbi. In autumn 2018, it signed a currency swap deal with Japan which was worth C¥200 billion (US$29 billion). At the same time, the Bank of China's Tokyo branch was named by the Japanese central bank as the clearing house for yuan transactions in Japan.[42] The deal was hugely significant. Here we saw the world's second- and third-largest economies joining hands. At the same time, China is actively pushing to conclude a significant free trade agreement involving 16 countries in the region, including China, Japan, India, Australia and New Zealand. If successful, the Regional Comprehensive Economic Partnership (RCEP) agreement will represent 50% of the world's population and 32% of global GDP. Mutual trade among members accounts for 28% of world trade.[43]

India has also signalled that it is open to other options. In July 2019, India agreed a $10 billion defence deal, buying military equipment from Russia. Although it was recorded as 10 billion *dollars* (old habits die hard) this was not strictly the case. The first payments are slated to be settled in rubles and rupees via a new payment mechanism.[44] At present Delhi is saying this will only go ahead if President Trump agrees not to impose sanctions in retaliation. However, it is still hugely significant that these types of deal have even been discussed. A year or so ago, it would have been out of the question.

Going for gold

It is not just paper money that is the focus of moves away from the dollar. In fact, one of the main beneficiaries of the nervousness about the future of the premier reserve currency is gold. Gold has long had a reputation as a safe haven in tough times, since it can hold its value when everything else collapses around it. It is the commodity that investors always return to in an uncertain environment of high inflation, debt or when asset bubbles burst. Sure enough, World Gold Council figures show that central banks purchased gold worth a record $15.7 billion in the first six months of 2019. The banks, led by Poland, Russia and China, have bought 374 tonnes of gold, the largest acquisition of gold ever recorded in the first half of a year, since the end of the gold standard. Indeed, central bank demand accounted for nearly one-sixth of all gold bought in that period.[45] The pattern builds on 2018 trends, when central banks bought more gold than at any other time since the gold standard ended in 1971.

The shift towards gold has been underlined by the European Central Bank decision in July 2019 to drop the 20-year-old Central Bank Gold Agreement (CBGA) that limited sales of gold.[46] Institutions are no longer *selling* gold in large volumes, they are now acquiring it in record amounts. The 1999 agreement was brought in to limit sporadic sales, often conducted in secret, which had driven down prices and undermined gold's status as a stable reserve asset. In a clear sign of how reliable, stable and dependable investors now view the precious metal, the price of gold barely moved following the CBGA announcement.

There is now ample evidence that the USA is heading towards the vertical or 'sudden' stage of the parabolic curve; whether it is ready to acknowledge the fact, or actively intervene, remains to be seen. What we all need to be thinking about is: what next? How can we protect ourselves from the inevitable fall-out from the dollar's reduced status on the world stage?

FIVE

The Great Devaluation

It would be nice to write that the USA is not going to let the dollar collapse without a really good fight. Unfortunately, efforts thus far to ensure the Mighty Greenback lives up to its name have been modest at best. So-called 'monetary normalisation' efforts have involved gradual shifts in interest rates and efforts to stop the run-off rate of bonds, which in effect calls a halt to quantitative tightening. The initiatives are very much of a stop-and-start nature, and are brought to an abrupt halt whenever there are any strong signs of disinflation, disorderly markets or a slow-down in the jobs market.

President Trump has been characteristically vocal about wanting a weaker dollar, correctly observing that the weakness in foreign currencies and corresponding strength of the dollar is a drag on the US economy. If the currency were weaker, exports would be cheaper for overseas buyers, giving the USA a competitive advantage. It would also boost corporate earnings, since around 40% of the revenue from America's largest corporations comes from outside the country. But weakening a currency, or devaluation, is a significant undertaking.

Let us forget for a moment the massive *volte-face* this would require from the US president. He was, after all, hugely critical of China's move to weaken the renminbi to undermine the effects of the US/China trade tariff war. Ditto the European Central Bank's announcement that it might restart the stimulus programme to bolster European economies, which prompted accusations of unfairly pushing down the euro. There is likely to be huge resistance to weakening the dollar from many quarters in the USA, amid fears this would lead to soaring inflation, further denting an already weak position. Plus, devaluation can, in the long term, lead to lower productivity. US firms might feel less incentive to cut costs, since they could rely on the weaker dollar to provide competitive edge. Ordinary citizens would feel the pinch too, particularly when they went abroad on holiday.

Aside from all the (most likely very heated) arguments for and against, there is the thorny issue that it is not that easy for the USA to weaken the dollar because of its role as a currency reserve. The currency markets are huge: every day more than $5 trillion changes hands in the market, $4 trillion of which involves the dollar.

The fact is, the USA just does not have the firepower to weaken its currency at will. To explain why, let's compare its situation to China. China can devalue the renminbi because it has the vast reserves and considerable freedom of manoeuvre of its People's Bank of China. The central bank publishes the price for the currency on a daily basis and dictates the amount of trading. If the situation should warrant it, the PBOC is able to print new currency if the exchange rate gets too high. Alternatively, there are $3 trillion in reserves that can be deployed if there is any danger of the currency getting too weak.

Hardly surprisingly, the USA operates in an entirely different way. The government has a limited capacity to intervene in the financial markets, via the Exchange Stabilization Fund, which is controlled by the Treasury Secretary. The fund has around $100 billion in buying power. This sounds a lot, but is clearly nowhere close to the Chinese reserves. The only way the Exchange Stabilization Fund can be enlarged is through authority from Congress, which is not easy to obtain in the current bi-partisan mood.

Orderly and disorderly devaluation

There is precedent for orderly devaluation. In the past, when the USA wanted to change the value of the dollar, it had to coordinate efforts with a number of other countries. This is what happened in 1985, after a sharp, extended run upwards saw the dollar rise by around 50%

against other currencies.[47] The Plaza Accord was prompted when concerns about the surge in the dollar contributing to a growing US trade deficit, against a backdrop of Congress calling for protectionist measures, promoted a meeting at New York's Plaza Hotel, where the US, the UK, Japan, West Germany and France were represented. The dollar subsequently dropped by 40% in the following two years. While the Plaza Accord has been held up as one of the most successful episodes in coordinated exchange rate intervention, the countries involved were all strategic allies of the USA. Few commentators would talk up the chances of China being convinced to let its currency strengthen to bail out the USA, particularly after the war of words in recent years.

The alternative to an orderly and controlled weakening of the dollar is the opposite scenario: a disorderly, uncontrolled and most likely extremely rapid devaluation. Here, we would see a drop of, perhaps, 50% in a very short space of time. The likelihood of such an event increases by the day, since the longer a government runs deficits, the higher the debt and the higher the interest rates it has to offer to persuade the market to take more of its bonds. The payments to service the debt swallow up an ever-greater share of available tax revenues. Sooner or later, at least some investors will wake up with a start and realise the whole house of cards is at risk. The present situation is completely unsustainable. When investors wake up, they will begin a rapid sell-off of bonds and, once other investors realise what is going on, they will scramble to get out too. Before long, the sell-off will become a rout. Interest rates would be driven up sharply and with foreign investors amongst those liquidating their positions the dollar would collapse.

A fair number of investors will most likely be caught entirely off-guard when the panic starts. Anyone left holding a large amount of dollars, which of course means almost every country in the world, will suffer catastrophic losses. No amount of QE, QT or whatever monetary normalisation process succeeds these strategies, will be able to see off what will be a cascading wave of defaults. Institutional investors will be at a high risk of insolvency; indeed, the entire global financial system will enter a very perilous era. The international community will think twice about using the dollar in any circumstances. Bond holders will shun dollar-denominated claims. There is no doubt that this could be the tipping point at which the dollar loses its status as the premier reserve currency.

Ah, you may say: the Fed will step in before the situation deteriorates that far. They will intervene to support the dollar. It is a fair supposition. However, the theory suffers from the same problem as the modern equivalent of the Plaza Accord. To explain, let's play this scenario out. Under normal circumstances, the obvious defensive measure would be to try to achieve price stability and target employment growth. In this case, that is not an option. There is no time. The alternative is for the Fed to go to the foreign exchange markets and buy up dollars. This would make it more expensive for speculators to bet against the dollar by raising interest rates. Such an intervention might work: market panics do not last forever. If handled skilfully, this sort of intervention by the Fed might pause a run on the dollar. However, the entire strategy is reliant on one thing: the help of America's friends and allies. After all, the Fed's options are limited by the reserves of foreign currencies that it holds, which are small in comparison to the scale of the problem. A similar situation occurred in the 1960s, when America had to call upon assistance from Germany, France and the UK to maintain the dollar's peg to gold. On that occasion, the growing economies of Europe and Japan found themselves rapidly accumulating dollars and there were concerns over the value of these holdings, particularly if the markets had shifted. In those days, the market was friendlier to the dollar; cooperation, or at least obligation, was seen as key. If the same situation occurred now, America would need to seek agreements from China, Russia and the oil-exporting nations of the Middle East. It would hope that self-interest would discourage any of these countries from pursuing a policy that would damage its own competitiveness. There is a shared interest in keeping the global system stable. But how long would negotiations take when the parties involved have such different outlooks? We do not have the luxury of time here.

Let us assume that the immediate risk of a complete dollar collapse can somehow be contained; that the various Jackson Hole-style meetings bear fruit and a Plan B is swiftly brought to bear. The scene is set for investors to pile into other currencies. But would this avert disaster? Investor demand would drive up the value of these other currencies, rendering the owners of those currencies less competitive on the world stage, and probably force them to borrow more; falling competitiveness means rising unemployment.

Whatever way the scenario plays out, there is now absolutely no doubt that the dollar is in a very perilous position indeed.

SIX

Mar-a-Lago Gold

A fter all that has been said about the USA's own role in the dollar crisis, either through carelessness or benign neglect, it seems ironic that the potential salvation might emerge from those shores. Even more remarkable, is the fact that the solution is being advocated by no less than President Trump himself. And the proposed key to getting the global economy back on track? A return to the gold standard.

Judy Shelton, the economist picked by Trump to govern the Federal Reserve in July 2019, is a long-term proponent of tying the value of the dollar to gold and it appears she has advocated the idea to the president. Indeed, her call for a new Bretton Woods conference, perhaps to be held at Mar-a-Lago, seems to confirm this. A return to the gold standard would be the focus of the putative discussions at Trump's resort in Palm Beach, Florida. In an article in the journal of the Cato Institute, a libertarian think tank, Shelton laid out the reasoning behind her proposals. She wrote:

> 'We have not had a rules-based international monetary system since President Nixon ended the Bretton Woods agreement in August 1971. Today there are compelling reasons – political, economic, and strategic – for President Trump to initiate the establishment of a new international monetary system.'[48]

Shelton wrote what many central banks and economists are now coming around to thinking: the lack of any rules-based monetary system has fuelled growing problems in the free trade system which are now insurmountable. The obvious gaps between monetary policy and the genuine demands of individual economies are now so out of synch something drastic has to be done. We need international monetary reform and a return to the gold standard, which worked so effectively before, seems like one of the most sensible solutions.

Let us set aside the fact that the chance of a Bretton Woods-style conference at Mar-a-Lago are slim right now. The current protectionist environment characterised by bitter trade disputes is not conducive to such summits. It is highly likely that things will come to a head before an acceptable approach can be found and a Mar-a-Lago gold standard become a reality. In the meantime, to help you get one step ahead of this scenario, I would like to rehearse the arguments for and against bringing back the gold standard.

First and foremost, we need gold because, as indicated at the beginning of this book, it is the only way to achieve truly stable money. If the dollar is linked to gold once again, at a stroke this would insulate it from the economic volatility and monetary crises that are linked to fiat money.

Under a gold standard prices will rise and fall, responding naturally to changes in supply and demand, but the recent Fed policies will no longer be necessary, and so the artificial distortions brought about by them will fall away. In other words, money will fulfil its legitimate purpose as a facilitator of transactions, with much less impediment or interference. This will, in turn, encourage commerce because businesses and government will not constantly be having to guess what new central bank initiative will move the goalposts on trade next.

As we have seen here, if you leave decisions about the value and supply of money to bureaucrats, the system gets out of synch. Each new decision adds to the weight of the previous one, so the disparity just widens. The gold standard takes this decision-making out of the hands of bureaucrats. The role of central banks will switch to one where the focus is to maintain a stable gold price. When there is a gold standard, the price of gold is like a barometer.

It shows whether there is too much liquidity in the economy, or too little. It is a far more reliable barometer too, reflecting the impacts of the ever-changing actions and desires of the billions of people that live within the global markets. No second-guessing required. This is great because sophisticated equations and economic theory often fail to anticipate what people actually do, which is why decisions based on them are regularly wrong.

Under a gold standard, the cost of money will be higher than it is today, with interest remaining stubbornly low. However, the Fed will have less freedom to artificially suppress interest rates with price control measures. As a result, credit and capital will be more accessible. Businesses will more often be able to find loans at an affordable cost, which will be a welcome change from an environment where SMEs struggle to get any sort of credit. This, in turn, will stimulate the economy.

Perhaps one of the most significant arguments in favour of reintroducing the gold standard is that it will make those in charge more accountable. Governments will not simply be able to run the printing presses to pay for grand promises and win votes. That sort of hugely damaging profligacy will no longer be a practical option. Policies that require funding will require public support because they will have to be paid for via borrowing and/or taxation. When spending plans have consequences this encourages restraint. It certainly moves things away from a time when policies favoured certain small sections of the population while ignoring the needs of the majority.

Judy Shelton is not alone in championing a new gold standard. The idea is beginning to gain support from other powerful voices. Former Federal Reserve Chairman Alan Greenspan is a prominent supporter of the gold standard and has stood solidly by his assertions that the debt crisis could be averted if the USA returned to it.[49]

There will, of course, be objectors to the idea of returning to the gold standard. Previous suggestions of the idea have not been universally applauded by economists. In one Initiative on Global Markets Forum, where economists voted overwhelmingly against the idea of re-embracing the gold standard, Nobel laureate Richard Thaler questioned the very idea of the underlying principle, asking: *why tie to gold? Why not 1982 Bordeaux?*[50]

The hostility is down to long-held myths about gold, which seem to stubbornly endure, even today. Detractors will tell you that there is 'not enough gold in the world', or that the 'price is too volatile'. There have even been suggestions that it caused the Great Depression. None of this is true. Let me bust a few of those myths here. I'll start with the wine.

Six myths

Myth 1: It doesn't need to be gold. Why not 1982 Bordeaux?

It is true that many commodities through history have been used as money, including mackerel. However, the most successful by far has been gold, which quite simply retains its value more effectively than anything else. It is indestructible: you can grind it, smash it or melt it, but you will not be able to destroy it. It does not pass its peak, or get drunk by connoisseurs; or suffer from the problems associated with many other commodities. Compared to most, it packs considerable value into a small amount of space and is easy to transport and store.

Myth 2: A gold standard is too rigid and does not provide enough money for a growing economy

Gold is far less rigid than many critics think. Contrary to the common perception, a monetary base tied to gold can grow, or shrink, in response to demand. Why? Because the quantity of money (base money) is variable. It is the variability in the quantity of money that allows it to be maintained at the gold (or dollar) parity. If you look at the Fed balance sheets while they were on the gold standard, they varied a great deal. In the USA, base money in 1900 was 163 times what it had been in 1775. During the same period, the quantity of gold in the world increased by a factor of 1.8.[51]

It is completely wrong to say a fixed gold price would hold back economic growth by tying a government's hands when it comes to increasing the money supply. (Is that even a completely bad thing? Arguably, a lack of checks and balances on growth is what got us into trouble in the first place.) A gold standard would allow the money supply to expand naturally, but equally importantly, it would not restrict the supply of dollars.

What if a major crisis occurred, though? By this, I mean a major financial panic that demanded an emergency injection of liquidity. In this case, we could simply follow the precedent of the Bank of England, which introduced the concept of being a lender of last resort way back in the 1860s. The Federal Reserve could easily step in and fulfil the same function if required. It should also be noted that such an event is considerably less likely under the more stabilising conditions of a gold standard.

Myth 3: The gold standard caused the Great Depression

As any student of history will tell you, the Great Depression in the USA followed a period in which the economy expanded rapidly: the 1920s. The New York Stock Exchange became a scene of reckless speculation into stocks on which everyone from tycoons to janitors poured their cash. The party abruptly ended when production began to decline, unemployment rose and consumer spending slowed. So, where does gold fit in to all of this? Well, the anti-gold narrative says the USA was slow to raise interest rates to cool the over-heated stock market because it feared a run on gold in the UK. This is, sadly, a somewhat selective view of the history books.

One of the reasons that gold is cited in this scenario is because of the decision of Winston Churchill to fix gold parity following the First World War. He failed to take into account the inflation in the pound sterling that had financed Britain's war effort, and fixed gold parity at the level that had been in place for the previous 200 years. (Isaac Newton, Master of the Mint, formally fixed the price of gold in 1717 at the rate of three pounds, seventeen shillings and ten-and-one-halfpence to an ounce.) An unnecessary and damaging inflation ensued, but this was not because of a flaw in the gold standard. It was a mistake made in returning to pre-war parity.

A more likely contender to blame for causing the US stock market bubble was the Smoot–Hawley Tariff Act, which proposed introducing unprecedented protectionist policies in the USA, imposing an average of 60% duty on over 3,000 import items. When it looked certain that the unpopular Bill would pass through Congress, it triggered a stock market collapse. The markets briefly rallied when it appeared the Bill was faltering, but the slide resumed as soon as it was certain it would pass. Hardly surprisingly, countries outside the USA panicked too, as they saw what was once a growing market being snatched away. The Act set off a worldwide trade war which was said to have been as damaging to many economies as the First World War. What followed was a pattern of massive tax hikes worldwide.

Ah, critics may counter, but when the UK came off the gold standard in 1931, the downturn ended. Again, this is not true. The devaluation did give a little boost, as devaluations can do, but it actually went on to escalate the already bitter trade war. More than twenty countries followed the UK with devaluations, which were very damaging to an already global fragile economy. The experience is in great part what led to the Allies being so open to getting together at Bretton Woods in 1944 to make sure such a slump did not happen again. It is no coincidence that they willingly chose a new gold-based international monetary system to achieve this.

Myth 4: Gold shows too much price volatility. We will be worse off

Opponents to gold point to the large differences in price in recent years as proving that it is too volatile to be relied upon. During the 2008 global financial crisis, for example, the gold price rose from $850 per Troy ounce to $1,900 per Troy ounce; a 131% increase in value.[52] The argument is that if the Fed were to fix the price of gold on a given day, and then demand for gold changed dramatically, this would wreak havoc on the economy. Likewise, if the Fed pegged the rate too low, people would want to trade their dollars for gold and that would force the Fed to raise interest rates to make gold less attractive. Detractors add that the fluctuating price of gold is disastrous for overseas markets, too. This is because, even if the Fed correctly guessed the price of gold, it would still have to make adjustments based on the economies of the USA's trading partners. After all, if the dollar is growing in value but another currency is declining, yet both are pegged to gold, there will have to be some inflation, or deflation of a currency, or an adjustment in exchange rate.

Let's start with the easy one. If two currencies are pegged to gold, in theory their exchange rates are fixed relative to one another, but actually the markets will cause them to vary – just as the markets do with no gold standard. Regarding the volatility, well that misunderstands how the gold standard works. The price of gold reflects supply and demand and linking to it affects neither of those fundamentals. This is why it is well known as a refuge for investors seeking something more solid at difficult times. The reason why the price of gold has been steadily rising is in response to all the uncertainties documented in this book. If the dollar was sound, there would be much less demand for gold and the price would not have been driven up.

Myth 5: Adopting the gold standard makes nations vulnerable to runs on the gold supply/speculators

To start with the potential for runs on the supply: gold in and of itself does not constitute wealth; gold's power lies in its effectiveness as a measure. A gold-based system would work even if a country does not own an ounce of the precious metal, but of course it would need to hold reserves to meet potential demand. A run presents problems for a country, whether it is a run on a commodity or a run on its currency.

As for speculators, gold does not need to introduce additional vulnerability, as long as individual countries defend their currencies. The spectre of City speculators making a killing by making bets on weak positions is a sad fact of modern life. It seems that every time there is a financial crisis, there are always a handful of speculators walking away with billions as the markets collapse around us. The evolution in technology has hugely helped this syndrome because a massive amount of data can be processed, meaning the speculators have vast resources at their fingertips to work out whether, and how, to make their audacious bets. It is possible to defend gold-backed currencies, nonetheless. How? By reducing reserves to buy the national currency and then maintaining its exchange rate by reducing the monetary base. There is precedent here. In 2009, when the Russian ruble came under speculative attack, Russia started buying rubles. Its monetary base declined and the attack failed. It is possible to mount a similar defence against a speculative attack on any gold-backed currency.

Myth 6: Setting a fixed dollar/gold ratio is anti-free market

Having got this far in the book, I would hope that most readers would agree that letting the market grow unchecked and simply printing more money as required is, ultimately, an unsustainable strategy. However, a gold standard does not mean the market is no longer free. In fact, I would argue that a gold standard is essential for free and *fair* markets.

None of these myths have been plucked from fresh air. A quick Google search will reveal many people who remain cynical about the role of gold and in particular who harbour a widespread uneasiness about any return to the gold standard. I suspect that with so many dissenting voices about gold, it is likely that nothing will really change until markets collapse (which is what will most likely happen). Hopefully the arguments for a gold standard will then be carefully examined with an open mind.

Setting the standard

Something that may help to swing support the gold standard's way when the time comes is the fact that those who advocate it most strongly, such as Trump advisor Judy Shelton, are discussing a *new* type of gold standard. One that is applicable to the twenty-first century. The idea is to move away from the classic gold standard model, where countries defined their currencies as worth a specified weight of gold. The new iteration would also be a step forward from the gold exchange standard that succeeded the classic model, under which only the US dollar was defined directly in terms of the precious metal, and other currencies were tightly pegged to the dollar.

Under new proposals for a gold standard, gold becomes strictly a yardstick of value, doing away with the need for nations to physically hold gold supplies. The dollar would be pegged to gold at an agreed price per ounce and the Federal Reserve would use its tools, primarily open market operations, to keep the value of the dollar close to the current value of that quantity of gold. Thus, if the market price moved above that level, the Fed would intervene in the open market, selling bonds to try to extract reserves from the banking system until gold reverted back to the agreed price. Likewise, if the price sunk below the target price, the Fed would buy back US government bonds, which would put money back into the banking system. Under this new standard there should be no benefit for speculators in attacking the system by buying up supplies of gold, because it is not necessary to hold gold for the system to work.

The big challenge to this system is agreeing the gold/dollar ratio. Setting it too low risks delivering a damaging deflationary shock to the economy at, arguably, a time when it is extremely vulnerable. The calculation will need to be based on the M1 money supply of the USA, China, Japan, and the euro zone, which is currently in excess of $24 trillion. (The M1 money supply is composed of physical currency and coin, or assets that can most quickly be converted to cash.) The same countries also hold around 33,000 tons of gold. Advocates maintain that a successful gold standard needs 40% gold backing to maintain confidence.[53] Forty per cent of £24 trillion is $9.6 trillion in gold, the amount believed to be required to support the money supply. To set the gold price, you would take the 33,000 tons of gold and divide it by that $9.6 trillion figure. This method implies a gold price of more than $9,000 per ounce. There have been forecasts that with the global M1 supply continually growing, this method could produce figures of closer to £10,000 per ounce.

Careful thought also needs to be given to the phasing-in of the new monetary system. There could, for example, be a programme run over a year, working towards the date of the conversion to a gold standard. Bringing the system in over a time would help the markets prepare for the return to a gold-based system. This period would also give financial institutions and investors breathing room to alter their investment strategies based on the new environment of more stable money. Any return to the gold standard would have to be written into law, with a provision to prevent the Fed from manipulating interest rates.

Under the new gold standard, it is highly likely most countries will peg their currency to dollars, if only for convenience. Aside from anything, it makes trading with the USA much easier. Of course, if any nation wished to attach its currency directly to gold, rather than the dollar, it could do so. The outcome would be the same: stable currencies and stable exchange rates.

Whichever side of the fence economists sit, whether for, or against, the gold standard, everyone is agreed on one thing: we are at a pivotal moment. The current monetary system which allows governments to actively distort exchange rates while angrily decrying trade protectionism elsewhere has caused huge and damaging distortions in the market. It affords central banks unfair powers to channel the benefits of their monetary policy decisions to wealthy investors, while ignoring average savers. The strategy has created a boom in 'cheap' government borrowing. None of this comes close to the 'free market' ideal espoused when Nixon axed the gold standard in 1971. The time to act is now.

Afterword

If you have read this book thoroughly and are as alarmed as you should be about the current state of the dollar, you are most likely asking yourself: what now? The collapse of the paper money system will be a significant shock to the economies of the world. There will be many losers and hardly any winners. I strongly suspect that the majority of the globe is relying on the powers-that-be to come up with something at the eleventh hour. There are, after all, a great many examples where exactly this has happened. We got through the Great Depression, saw off the Cold War and found a way to alleviate potential financial disaster following the 2008 global credit crisis. Yet, while there is ample evidence of nations triumphing over adversity, there is also an abundance of examples of the sudden collapse of kingdoms and complex social systems that had stood strong for centuries. Now is certainly not the time for complacency. The power of the dollar is under threat on a number of fronts, from debt-to-GDP ratios, escalating trade conflicts, slower recovery from the financial crisis than in previous crises, a declining labour force and a rapid increase in pensioners, to stagnant real wages and income inequality. Taken alone, any of these trends would be a real threat. Together, they represent an unprecedented peril.

Paper money systems are inherently unstable. Over time, they can destabilise a weak economy and ultimately lead to economic chaos. We are at that point right now. Whatever measures are taken to extend the life of the current system will only delay the inevitable. An even-greater crisis will certainly loom, and most likely not too far off the heels of the previous one. The lunacy of it all is: paper money has absolutely no advantages over inelastic, commodity money. Indeed, it has many disadvantages.

If, like me, your faith is low that governments/ central banks/stock markets will come up with a workable solution in time to prevent the forthcoming significant financial crisis, now is the time to act. Self-preservation should be the priority and you need to think how to best cushion yourself from what will be one of the most significant downturns in your lifetime, if not *the* most significant downturn.

Right now, no one can predict exactly when the wider population will become aware that something is very wrong. The consensus is that the crisis will spring to life abruptly, following the parabolic curve. It might be triggered by a catastrophic event such as a natural disaster, or pandemic, or something more man-made such as the collapse of a major bank. Perhaps a hostile force will attack the critical infrastructure of a major nation, using computer viruses. A catalyst like any of these scenarios (and others we may not even have imagined yet) could trigger a chain reaction where one system failure causes another and then another. There is little point dwelling on what the potential trigger will be for a dramatic downturn. Nor should you be wondering whether the world will work out a way around the crisis. Just know that there is little that central banks can really do. They cannot, for example, resort to printing money as they have in the past, because the balance sheets are still too bloated. Your energies are far better spent on planning ahead and protecting your assets from the vast instabilities in the monetary system that will ensue.

Even if the trigger event does not occur in the next year, or the one after that, the consensus is that growth will continue to slow markedly. As we saw, people are retiring in record numbers, at a time when low birth rates around the millennium mean that fewer young people are entering the workforce. Plus, levels of personal debt are increasing and so are student loan defaults.

In any scenario, the message is the same: if you have been an active investor in the past, you will now need to begin to think differently. Your goal is no longer to *get rich*. It is to *preserve what you have*. Clearly, traditional money-preservation policies such as sticking your cash into a savings account will not help you any more. There is zero point in parking your capital in a bank that pays little or no interest, thanks to the widespread policy of interest rate suppression. And what if financial institutions go to the wall, as seems likely if the disorderly devaluation we considered in chapter 5 is forced on the dollar?

It will probably come as no surprise to you that the number one recommendation when it comes to preserving wealth is to invest in gold. Gold has always come into its own during uncertain times. This is why we are already seeing the gold price edging up. It is a recognised safety net when there is any weakness in the global economy. Forget about stocks and bonds. They could lose their value and become all but worthless, if the next depression is anything like the Great Depression. Businesses could collapse, debtors default and the value of what is left be wiped out by inflation. Gold is the safest bet right now.

So, what do I do?

To get started, determine your available, investible assets. This sum does not include equity in your home or business, or other assets that you need on a day-to-day basis for your livelihood. Then, allocate 10% of your investible assets to physical gold.

While gold should not be viewed as an investment, it is highly likely that the price will rise considerably in a downturn. History has always shown this to be the case. If a new-style gold standard were to be adopted we saw in chapter 6 that it has been forecast that the price could become $10,000 or more per ounce.

Another defensive tactic is to move a proportion of your money into cash, or readily accessible accounts. This will help reduce the overall volatility of your portfolio and offer some deflation protection, since the real value of cash rises in a deflationary environment. Most importantly, cash allows you to be versatile. You will be able to pivot rapidly and take investment opportunities, should they arise. There will be bargains to be had as and when a financial crash occurs and asset values collapse.

If you have not already done so, you should reduce your exposure to high-valuation, rapid-growth tech stocks such as Facebook, Apple, Amazon, Netflix and Google (the so-called FAANG basket). These stocks top the list of stocks that are trading at more than ten times their annual revenues: a sure sign of over-inflation. You may see them gain in the short term, but they are well overdue for a significant fall once a real crisis begins. If you stick with FAANGS, you will see large losses when the correction kicks off. I would certainly recommend against a strategy of remaining nimble and alert, so you can sell stocks as late as possible before conditions shift. But do not hold on too long: events may occur so rapidly that they leave you behind.

To explain how a portfolio with 10% allocated to gold would protect you overall, let me share a calculation from author and gold expert James Rickards.[54] He assumes a portfolio allocation of

10% gold, 30% cash, and 60% equities. If, in an unlikely scenario, the gold price falls 20% in a financial crisis, the impact on the portfolio will be an overall 2% decline (20% × 10%). On the other hand, if the gold price does indeed rise to $10,000 (a 650% gain from the current gold price level) the overall boost to the portfolio is 65% (650% × 10%): a pretty impressive gain by any measure. Of course, you will need to take into account that the stock side to your portfolio is vulnerable to a financial crisis. For the purposes of this calculation, imagine stock price falls of 85%, which is what happened during the worst days of the Great Depression. With 60% of a portfolio in stocks, an 85% drop would produce an overall loss of just over 50% (85% × 60%). The gold gains outweigh the stock losses; meanwhile the 30% cash proportion probably holds its value. Your total wealth is not just preserved: it even increases by 15% (+65% − 50%). In a financial crisis as severe as the Great Depression, or even more so, this is an exceptional win. It will certainly stand out from the majority of portfolios which do not follow this strategy and might therefore face crippling losses. Indeed, investors who do not hold an allocation in gold face being wiped out when the current financial situation reaches crisis.

Whatever solutions the academic luminaries and central bankers *eventually* thrash out, it is unlikely to be anything close to the one we have today. The dollar's role as the premier reserve currency is all but over. The key to survival in the forthcoming collapse is not to dig a bunker and fill it with tinned goods. It is to invest in tangible assets such as gold, and keep liquid, to provide yourself with options. Gold is the only store of hard value, when value is what you will need in the tough months (or years) to come.

References

1   http://data.imf.org/?sk=E6A5F467-C14B-4AA8-9F6D
    -5A09EC4E62A4, accessed 11 November 2019. IMF:
    Currency composition of Official Foreign Exchange
    reserves.

2   www.bis.org/publ/work137.pdf, accessed 11 November
    2019. Barry Eichengreen and Kris Mitchener, 2003,
    'The Great Depression as a credit boom gone wrong',
    BIS Working Papers No. 137, Bank for International
    Settlements.

3   www.investopedia.com/news/when-fdr-abandoned-gold
    -standard/, accessed 11 November 2019. Mrinalini
    Krishna, 2017, 'When FDR abandoned the gold standard',
    Investopedia.

4   http://citeseerx.ist.psu.edu/viewdoc/download?doi=10
    .1.1.590.924&rep=rep1&type=pdf, accessed 11 November
    2019. Mark Harrison, 1998, 'The economics of World
    War II: an overview', in Harrison (ed.), *The Economics of
    World War II: Six Great Powers in International Comparison*
    (Cambridge: Cambridge University Press), pp. 1–42.

5   https://history.state.gov/milestones/1969-1976/nixon
    -shock, accessed 11 November 2019. US State Department,
    'Nixon and the end of the Bretton Woods system,
    1971–1973'.

6   www.visualcapitalist.com/12-stunning-visualizations
    -of-gold-bars-show-its-rarity, accessed 11 November 2019.
    Jeff Desjardins, 2015, '12 stunning visualizations of gold
    shows its rarity'.

7   www.newyorkfed.org/medialibrary/media/research
    /current_issues/ci16-1.pdf, accessed 12 November 2019.
    Linda Goldberg, 2010, 'Is the international role of the

dollar changing?', *Current Issues in Economics* 16/1 (New York: Federal Reserve Bank of New York).

8   https://moneyweek.com/513757/the-us-dollars-days -as-the-worlds-most-important-currency-are-numbered -its-official/, accessed 12 November 2019. John Stepek, 2019, 'The US dollar's days as the world's most important currency are numbered – it's official', *Money Week*, 27 August.

9   www.thebalance.com/what-is-forex-trading-3306253, accessed 12 November 2019. Kimberley Amadeo, 2018, 'Forex trading and how it determines the dollar's value', The Balance.com.

10   https://ec.europa.eu/eurostat/web/products-eurostat -news/-/DDN-20170824-1 accessed 12 November 2019. Eurostat, 2017, 'The EU, USA and China account for almost half of world trade in goods', 24 August.

11   www.bbc.co.uk/news/world-us-canada-45123607, accessed 12 November 2019. BBC, 2018, 'Trump doubles metal tariffs on Turkey as lira falls by 20%', 10 August.

12   www.thebalance.com/who-owns-the-u-s-national-debt -3306124, accessed 12 November 2019. Kimberley Amadeo, 2019, 'Who owns the US national debt?', The Balance.com.

13   George Soros, *The New Paradigm for Financial Markets* (New York: Hachette/Public Affairs, 2008).

14   www.cnbc.com/2016/06/13/12-trillion-of-qe-and-the -lowest-rates-in-5000-years-for-this.html, accessed 12 November 2019. Jeff Cox, 2016, '$12 trillion of QE and the lowest rates in 5,000 years. for this?', CNBC, 13 June.

15   www.bankofengland.co.uk/monetary-policy /quantitative-easing, accessed 12 November 2019. Bank of England, 'What is quantitative easing?'

16   www.schroders.com/en/insights/economics/the -longest-bull-market-in-history-in-five-charts/, accessed 12 November 2019. David Brett, 2018, 'The longest bull market in history: five charts that tell the story', Schroders, 22 August.

17   www.investopedia.com/why-the-corporate-debt-bubble -may-burst-sooner-than-you-think-4587446, accessed 12 November 2019. Mark Kolakowski, 2019, 'Why the corporate debt bubble may burst sooner than you think', *Investopedia*.

18   www.thebalance.com/is-the-real-estate-market-going -to-crash-4153139, accessed 12 November 2019. Kimberley

Amadeo, 2019, 'Is the real estate market going to crash?', The Balance.com.

19 www.cnbc.com/2018/09/21/the-student-loan-bubble .html, accessed 12 November 2019. Annie Nova, 2018, 'Despite the economic recovery, student debtors' "monster in the closet" has only worsened', CNBC, 13 September.

20 https://city.wsj.com/articles/e4a6d373-d13b-4de2-9be4 -436d36ob3ea2, accessed 12 November 2019. *Wall Street Journal*, 2017, 'Dollar stands strong a decade after the crisis', 27 November.

21 *Wall Street Journal*, 'Dollar stands strong'.

22 https://globalfinancialdata.com/the-century-of-inflation/, accessed 13 November 2019. Bryan Taylor, n.d., 'The century of inflation', Global Financial Data white paper.

23 https://en.wikipedia.org/wiki/Bernanke_doctrine, accessed 13 November 2019.

24 www.nytimes.com/2019/08/21/us/politics/deficit-will -reach-1-trillion-next-year-budget-office-predicts.html, accessed 13 November 2019. Jim Tankersley and Emily Cochrane, 2019, 'Budget deficit on path to surpass $1 trillion under Trump', *The New York Times*, 21 August.

25 www.reuters.com/article/us-usa-trade-china-bonds -explainer/explainer-will-china-dump-u-s-bonds-as -a-trade-weapon-not-so-fast-idUSKCN1SY0BS, accessed 13 November 2019. Richard Leong, 2019, 'Explainer: Will China dump U.S. bonds as a trade weapon? Not so fast', Reuters, 28 May.

26 IMF, *World Economic Outlook* July 2019.

27 *New York Times*, 'Budget deficit on path to $1 trillion'.

28 www.theguardian.com/business/2019/aug/05/markets -fall-sharply-amid-fears-of-full-scale-us-china-yuan -currency-war, accessed 13 November 2019. Richard Partington, 2019, 'US stocks suffer worst day of year as trade fears spook markets', *The Guardian*, 5 August.

29 www.bbc.co.uk/news/business-47862622, accessed 13 November 2019. BBC, 2019, 'US proposes tariffs on $11bn of EU products', 9 April.

30 www.theatlantic.com/politics/archive/2019/05/why -united-states-uses-sanctions-so-much/588625, accessed 13 November 2019. Kathy Gilsinan, 2019, 'A boom time for US sanctions', 3 May.

31   http://worldpopulationreview.com/countries/countries
      -by-national-debt, accessed 13 November 2019. World
      Population Review, 'Debt to GDP ratio by country 2019'.

32   https://news.usc.edu/143675/aging-u-s-population
      -unique-health-challenges, accessed 13 November 2019.
      Maya Meinert, 2018, 'Seniors will soon outnumber
      children, but the US isn't ready', USC News, 21 June.

33   www.pgpf.org/blog/2018/11/we-will-soon-be-spending
      -more-on-national-debt-interest-than-on-these-vital
      -programs, accessed 13 November 2019. Peter Peterson,
      2018, 'What is the National Debt costing us?', 29
      November.

34   www.thebalance.com/fed-rate-hike-impact-emerging
      -markets-4087480, accessed 13 November 2019. Justin
      Kuepper, 2019, '5 ways a Fed rate hike could impact
      emerging markets', The Balance.com, 14 August.

35   www.newsweek.com/ferguson-how-economic-weakness
      -endangers-us-76685, accessed 13 November 2019. Niall
      Ferguson, 2009, 'How economic weakness endangers the
      US', Newsweek, 27 November.

36   World Population Review, 'Debt to GDP ratio 2019'.

37   www.ft.com/content/360028ba-c702-11e9-af46
      -b09e8bfe60c0, accessed 14 November 2019. Brendan
      Greeley, 2019, 'Central bankers rethink everything at
      Jackson Hole', Financial Times, 25 August.

38   https://moneyweek.com/513757/the-us-dollars-days
      -as-the-worlds-most-important-currency-are-numbered
      -its-official, accessed 14 November 2019. John Stepek,
      2019, 'The US dollar's days as the world's most important
      currency are numbered – it's official', Money Week, 27
      August.

39   www.reuters.com/article/us-eu-juncker-euro
      /eus-juncker-wants-bigger-global-role-for-euro
      -idUSKCN1LS0BK, accessed 14 November 2019. Reuters,
      2018, 'EU's Juncker wants bigger global role for euro', 12
      September.

40   https://blog.sfox.com/bitcoin-at-136-000-can-it-become
      -the-new-gold-standard-ee98b11aacfc, accessed 14
      November 2019. SFOX, 2018, 'Bitcoin at $136,000: can it
      become the new gold standard?', 26 April.

41   www.reuters.com/article/us-forex-reserves/us-dollar
      -share-of-global-currency-reserves-at-lowest-since-2013
      -imf-data-idUSKBN1WF1IO, accessed 14 November 2019.

Saqib Iqbal Ahmed, 2019, 'US dollar share of global currency reserves at lowest since 2013: IMF data', Reuters, 30 September.

42 www.scmp.com/economy/china-economy/article /2170426/china-and-japan-sign-us29-billion-currency -swap-forge-closer, accessed 14 November 2019. Sidney Leng, 2018, 'China and Japan sign US$29 billion currency swap to forge closer ties', *South China Morning Post*, 26 October.

43 www.nbr.org/publication/rcep-negotiations-and-the -implications-for-the-united-states, accessed 14 November 2019. Takashi Terada, 2018, 'RCEP Negotiations and the Implications for the United States', National Bureau of Asian Research, 20 December.

44 www.thehindubusinessline.com/economy/policy /defence-deals-india-russia-agree-on-new-payment -mode-to-skirt-us-sanctions/article28436297.ece, accessed 14 November 2019. Bloomberg, 2019, 'Defence deals: India, Russia agree on new payment mode to skirt US sanctions', The Hindu Business Line, 15 July.

45 www.ft.com/content/b62ebb1a-b3a6-11e9-bec9 -fdcab53d6959, accessed 14 November 2019. Central banks make record $15.7bn gold purchases, FT, August 1 2019

46 www.reuters.com/article/europe-cenbank-gold/update -1-europes-central-banks-ditch-20-year-old-gold-sales -agreement-idUSL8N24R4YO, accessed 14 November 2019. Francesco Canepa and Peter Hobson, 2019, 'Europe's central banks ditch 20-year-old gold sales agreement', Reuters, 26 July.

47 www.marketwatch.com/story/a-1985-global-deal-to -weaken-the-dollar-offers-a-road-map-to-ending-the -trade-war-2019-08-08, accessed 14 November 2019. William Watts, 2019, 'Why a 1985 global deal to weaken the dollar offers a road map to ending the trade war', MarketWatch, 10 August.

48 https://www.cato.org/cato-journal/springsummer-2018 /case-new-international-monetary-system, accessed 14 November 2019. Judy Shelton, 2018, 'The case for a new international monetary system', *Cato Journal* 38(2).

49 https://markets.businessinsider.com/commodities/news /greenspan-defends-gold-standard-infrastructure-2017 -2-1001758059-1001758059, accessed 14 November 2019. Akin Oyedele, 2017, 'Greenspan: The US cannot afford to

spend on infrastructure like it wants to because it's not on the gold standard', Markets Insider, 16 February.

50 www.igmchicago.org/surveys/gold-standard, accessed 14 November 2019. Initiative on Global Markets, 2012, 'Gold Standard', 12 January.

51 www.forbes.com/sites/nathanlewis/2018/06/01/five -gold-standard-notions-that-just-arent-true/#2ba4fe5246f7, accessed 14 November 2019. Nathan Lewis, 2018, 'Five gold standard notions that just aren't true', *Forbes*, 1 June.

52 www.moneymetals.com/precious-metals-charts/gold -price, accessed 14 November 2019. Money Metals Exchange, 'Price of gold per ounce live & historical charts'.

53 www.bullionvault.com/gold-news/gold-allocation -051120181, accessed 14 November 2019. James Rickards, 2018, 'Gold and 90% other stuff', Bullion Vault, 11 May.

54 James Rickards, *Aftermath, Seven secrets of wealth preservation in the coming chaos* (Penguin Random House, 2019).

Acknowledgments

I would like to say a big thank you to my business partners Neil Barrett and Adam Matich, who continue to patiently listen to my views on the future of our global economy and the roles of fiat currencies and gold in particular. You have both been brilliant sounding boards and have greatly helped me order my thoughts for this book. Thank you also to Teena Lyons, who has assisted me in editing The Last Dollar into shape.

My biggest vote of thanks must go to my wife Claire, who has always been, and remains, a massive support to me and our children, Niamh and Max.

The Author

 Phil Taylor-Guck's career has been fuelled by curiosity. After discovering an early entrepreneurial flair and with an insatiable curiosity for finding better ways of doing things, he has pursued a number of successful business opportunities. This led Phil (known as PTG) to create his own investment group and since doing so he has invested in international companies which work in technology, venture capital, private equity and real estate. A hunger to learn more about commodities, and the technology around the process of

delivering them, led him to start to scrutinise the world of finance; a sector he concluded was riddled with fatal flaws. Phil is now CEO of RTK International Holdings, a financial services and commodities trading group, spanning four continents and headquartered in Hong Kong.

www.rtkinternational.com
http://taylor-guck.co.uk
🐦 @philtaylorguck

Printed in Great Britain
by Amazon